DANA

WHITE

ULTIMATE FIGHTING

QUOTES

EDITED BY

NATHAN CAIRNS

Book design by Nathan Cairns
Copy editing by Ananda Djatschenko

natecairns@gmail.com

Printed in the United States of America

ISBN – 1453896554

"UFC will be the biggest sport in the world by 2020."

-Dana White

INTRODUCTION

When UFC President Dana White talks, people sit up and listen. Not only is he the most recognized and influential man in Mixed Martial Arts, he's also without question one of the most polarizing and enigmatic figures in the world of sports. He's brash, combative and profane yet he's in firm command of a billion dollar enterprise. He displays a ruthless, take-no-prisoners approach to detractors yet is exceptionally candid and friendly to his millions of loyal UFC fans. He has no formal business education yet it was his vision and street smarts that transformed the UFC from a debt-ridden, underground spectacle into a highly profitable, world-wide phenomenon. Love him or hate him, it would be hard to argue that anyone's opinion in MMA matters more than Dana White's.

In DANA WHITE: ULTIMATE FIGHTING QUOTES, I've offered up a generous helping of his most memorable quips, one-liners, rants, jibes and observations. All are delivered in the

same entertaining, no-holds-barred, profane-fueled style that has become synonymous with one of the most popular and controversial figures in sports today.

Nathan Cairns

DANA
WHITE

ULTIMATE FIGHTING

QUOTES

ULTIMATE FIGHTER

"Do you wanna be a fucking fighter?"

-To 'The Ultimate Fighter 1' reality show contestants

BIG

"The company is worth about $2.5 billion... I've been saying this since day one, and people really thought I was a lunatic, that this could be the biggest sport in the world. What I'm surprised about is how fast this has happened. We haven't even scratched the surface for how big this thing is going to be."

-On the phenomenal growth of the UFC

STREET FIGHT

"If you take four street corners, and on one they're playing baseball, on another they're playing basketball and on the other, street hockey. On the fourth corner, a fight breaks out. Where does the crowd go? They all go to watch the fight."

-On the universal appeal of fighting

HOOKED

"If you come to a live event...you're hooked, you're in. It is the greatest live sporting event you will ever see."

-On UFC live events

OLD SCHOOL

"Boxing is your fathers' sport."

-On the decline of boxing

FRIES WITH THAT?

"These idiots pop up and they start throwing all this money around, and they think they're going to come out and go head to head and compete with the UFC. It'd be like me starting a fast-food joint saying 'I'm going to take down McDonald's'."

-On the now defunct MMA promotion, Elite XC

SAFETY FIRST

"Do you know how many deaths there has been in the UFC over the last 15 years – zero. Do you know how many serious injuries there has been in the UFC over the last 15 years – zero. Badminton probably can't even say that."

-On the safety record of the UFC

TURNING POINT

"I knew at the end of that fight that we'd all won."

-On 'The Ultimate Fighter 1 Finale' bout between Stephan Bonnar and Forrest Griffin

BEYOND BORDERS

"If I put two guys in the Octagon and have them fight, that crosses language barriers, ethnic barriers, everything."

-On the international appeal of the UFC

BEYOND BORDERS II

"I take two guys and put them in an octagon and they can use any martial art they want – that transcends all culture barriers. Right now we are on some form of television in over 175 countries. We're all human beings and we all 'get' fighting."

- On the international appeal of the UFC

UNBEATABLE

"I'm going to outwork you, I'm going to stay up later than you are, I'm willing to do everything it takes to win and I'm going to beat you, and if you're not willing to do that, you're never going to fucking beat me, ever."

-To rival MMA promoters

SWEET DREAMS

"That's the kind of stuff we used to lay in bed and dream about."

-On the massive success of the UFC

JUDGES

"Don't leave it in the hands of the judges."

-On UFC judges

BUILT THIS INDUSTRY

"Everybody wants to come in and try to compete with us; we've been around for almost 20 years. I've been doing this for 10 years and we're the ones building the fucking industry. We have built this industry over the last nine years. Everybody else is following."

-On rival MMA promotions

BBQ'D

"We are in the business of promoting a sport; these fucking idiots are putting on a freak show, and the scumbags at Showtime have no issue putting it on the air. Kimbo Slice is not a fucking fighter. He got famous by showing up at barbecues and picking fights, and he lost half the fights he picked. And Roy Nelson? He's fatter than Rosie O'Donnell. How can you look like that and call yourself a professional fighter? I bet Roy Nelson was working the grill at the fucking barbecue Kimbo crashed."

-When asked how Elite XC would promote a Kimbo Slice vs. Roy Nelson bout

STICKS AND STONES

"Idiot, moron, retard, douche bag...liar"

-When asked his thoughts on Tito Ortiz

PROFITABLE

"This guy went on Howard Stern and said he was getting $200 thousand a fight, which was such a lie. Tito made $5.8 million in 2006...he's a moron. This guy talks about what a businessman he is, and he was on 'The Apprentice' and he doesn't know the difference between revenue and profit."

-On Tito Ortiz's salary complaints

WHAT, ME WORRY?

"Strike-farce is a little tiny show...who's Fedor going to fight, I got a bigger question for you, who's he going to fight, yeah Brett Rogers, what's Buck Rogers ranked?"

-On Fedor Emelianenko signing with Strikeforce

PITY THE FOOL

"Evans is thinking about kicking your ass, not about watching *The Love Boat* with his mother and how he could land the role of Isaac the bartender."

-On Quinton "Rampage" Jackson accepting a role in the A-Team movie instead of fighting Rashad Evans

DYSFUNCTIONAL

"I have never seen anything so unorganized, selfish and dysfunctional as boxing. It's a joke."

-On boxing

NFL

"There was a time when it was neck-and-neck. That time is over. There were times when we were in dogfights, but everybody needs to just concede and realize we're the fucking NFL. Period. End of story."

-On the UFC compared with rival MMA promotions

FROSTY

"Millen is a fucking clown that talks out of his ass and has no business; that guy is a nobody. When we did the big Fedor negotiations, you think he was in it? He wasn't even in it....That guy's full of shit. Tell him to go frost his fucking hair again and beat it."

-On former M1 Global executive, Jerry Millen

SERIOUSLY

"How can you put Strikeforce in the same fucking sentence as the UFC – seriously – with a straight face? How can you do it?"

-On rival MMA promotion, Strikeforce

FREAK SHOW

"The guy's an embarrassment; he's like a walking, talking freak show."

-On Tito Ortiz

THE GREATEST

"How can you call this guy the best in the world...When you say Fedor beat all the big names – that was back in PRIDE. You're talking what, four years ago? So wait a minute, maybe Muhammad Ali is the best pound-for-pound fighter in the world. By calling him best pound-for-pound in the world – that is insane."

-On top ranked heavyweight, Fedor Emelianenko

LOW BLOW

"Whoever came up with Houston Alexander's game plan ought to be kicked in the nuts for five minutes. I don't know if Kalib Starnes trained him for that fight or what the deal was, but it was horrible."

-On Houston Alexander's performance against Kimbo Slice

LOW BLOW II

"The fame and PR and movies and TV shows; it gets to you, it catches up with you and kicks you in the nuts.

-On Chuck Liddell falling asleep whilst a guest on the 'Good Morning Texas' TV show

PARASITE

"Scumbag Gary Shaw is a piece-of-shit dirt-bag who couldn't care less about our sport. He's one of the maggots I had to fight off who didn't believe in Mixed Martial Arts five years ago."

-On Elite XC President, Gary Shaw

PARASITE II

"Gary Shaw is a fucking loser…This guy is a low-level bottom feeder. He didn't like MMA a few years ago, but when he finally couldn't make money at boxing anymore, he came over to this sport to try to leech money out of it."

-On Elite XC President, Gary Shaw

LOST IN TRANSLATION

"He just fought Long Duck Dong."

-Referring to Korean fighter Hong Man Choi

LINE OF FIRE

"And when people say, 'Hey, these guys put their lives on the line,' that's a crock of shit. This sport is so safe. These guys have chosen to be fighters. These guys aren't going into Afghanistan. The U.S. military puts their life on the line. Police and fire-fighters walk into the line of fire...UFC fighters do not. These are smart guys with college educations. If they don't want to do this, go out and get a real job."

-On UFC fighter safety

CASH FOR RANKINGS

"Most of these goofy MMA sites...They get paid a lot of money from the smaller promotions. So they feel like they have to put some of their guys in some of these things. That's the way that works. That's why it makes me sick and drives me crazy..."

-On MMA websites allegedly skewing their fighter rankings for payment

CASH FOR RANKINGS II

"My biggest beef with a lot of these MMA websites is that these guys are for-profit websites. They're not fucking news sites."

-On MMA websites allegedly skewing their fighter rankings for payment

HEAD SPIN

"I'll throw you the fuck out of this gym so fucking fast your head will spin."

-To 'The Ultimate Fighter 1' reality show contestants

REALITY CHECK

"At first I was really pissed off that we got a reality show, I hate reality shows and I've never even watched one, I just never got the whole concept. But they're popular."

-On 'The Ultimate Fighter' reality TV show

FARMERS

"Whether they like it or not, they're a farm league."

-On the now defunct MMA promotion, Elite XC

YAKUZA

"They're going to have to kill me, that's what they're going to have to do. We're coming there no matter what. We're coming there. We're going to break through this thing. We're going to get past these dirty, sneaky, bad guys in Japan, and we're going to make it happen."

-On the UFC returning to Japan

CASH COW

"Another fucking joke from Gary Shaw. This fucker is so clueless that it's laughable. First he thought we protected our guys, which is bullshit. Then he gave us shit for matching up Brock against Frank Mir. Which would he rather us do? Obviously he's in favor of protecting guys since Kimbo doesn't seem to be fighting a good fighter anytime soon...It's clear that Gary is going to milk his YouTube cash cow for all he's worth but true fans know that Kimbo is a joke and he would get destroyed against any UFC Heavyweight. Maybe that moron Ken Shamrock will expose Kimbo and he'll go back to fighting guys at the local Burger King. Gary Shaw and his third rate promotion have no fucking credibility."

-On the Elite XC Kimbo Slice vs. Ken Shamrock match-up

BUSH LEAGUE

"Now, they're stuck with a bush league, C-level promotion that will probably be out of business next month..."

-On the Strikeforce post fight brawl that was broadcast live on CBS

BUSH LEAGUE II

"When have you seen anything remotely close to that happen at a UFC event? What kind of ridiculous commentary was that? That was an idiotic thing to say...That was just another example of how bush league they are."

-On CBS commentary during the Strikeforce post fight brawl

FINANCIAL ADVICE

"Hey Jared, you're $60 million in the hole, retard. Get over it."

-On Elite XC Vice-President, Jared Shaw

CAREER ADVICE

"Jeremy Lappen, the three-time loser ... you have a law degree. Go get a real fucking job. Your parents must be bummed out, spent all that money on a law degree and you're fucking around in MMA, trying to screw up this business. Go screw up somebody's fucking court case or go do something else."

-On Elite XC Head of Fight Operations, Jeremy Lappen

BUSINESS ADVICE

"Gary Shaw, if you think going to the ground is boring, and Jeremy Lappen and rapper, whatever-the-fuck-your-name-is, Shaw Junior, okay that's called Mixed Martial Arts, you fucking morons need to be in the kickboxing business."

-On Elite XC Management

HEART

"If Frank Mir can't bully you, his heart shrinks to the size of the Grinch's. If he can't take you down, his heart shrinks to the size of a pea..."

-On Frank Mir

NOT A FAN

"I actually watched the IFL once, and it was fucking painful."

-On the now defunct MMA promotion, the IFL

TEAM SPORTS

"The IFL doesn't faze me one bit. It's like team tennis. That didn't work, and team fighting definitely won't work. Nobody wants to see team fighting. They've got the Woodchucks vs. the Crazy Beavers. Is that what you want to see on a Saturday night? It's a retarded concept."

-On the now defunct MMA promotion, the IFL

NOT WELCOME

"It makes me sick to my stomach. I've been killing myself for ten years. I don't need scumbags like that in here blowing this for everybody."

-On the now defunct MMA promotion, Elite XC

CAN'T WIN

"The only thing that Tito has left in his career is his fight with me because other than that nobody gives a shit, the guy hasn't won a fight in years...Tito needs to fight for one of these other organizations because he can't win a fight in the UFC."

-On his feud with Tito Ortiz

NOT GOOD

"Tom Atencio is a fucking loser, he's not a good promoter and he's definitely not a good fighter..."

-Responding to a fight challenge from Affliction Vice-President Tom Atencio

JOKER

"Why would I fight this goof? He's neither a fighter nor a promoter. He's a fucking loser. That's all he is.... Let me tell you something, when I was $44 million in the hole, the last thing I was doing was leaving the office and going out to train for a joke of a fight...That's a complete joke."

-Responding to a fight challenge from Affliction Vice-President Tom Atencio

NO DEAL

"If I was sitting on Fedor's lap that deal wouldn't have gotten done. We went in there to do a deal, they didn't...It wouldn't have mattered if we flew to Russia and sat in his living room, we weren't getting a deal done that day."

-On Fedor Emelianenko not signing a UFC contract

NO DEAL II

"I've already come to the realization and everyone else needs to too; that Fedor doesn't want to fight the best guys in the world."

-On Fedor Emelianenko not signing a UFC contract

COUNTER OFFER

"Fedor is not a top ten heavyweight. He just got beat by a guy who couldn't cut it in the UFC...Tell you what, if he wants to sign with the UFC now, the previous contract where I offered him an insane amount of money is off the table. I'll give him a new contract, 20K to show and 20K to win. If he doesn't accept it, too bad."

-On Fedor Emelianenko's shock loss to Fabricio Werdum

THE THREE F'S

"...I've said this guy was a fake, a phoney and a farce and he proved it last weekend."

-On Fedor Emelianenko's shock loss to Fabricio Werdum

CANADA

"Canada is the Mecca for Mixed Martial Arts."

-On the popularity of MMA in Canada

CANADIANS

"...fucking Canada has the craziest fucking Mixed Martial Arts fans on the planet, everywhere we go, it doesn't matter where it is in the United States or in the UK, there are a million fucking Canadians there, going crazy..."

- On Canadian UFC fans

MURDERED

"Kimbo Slice would get murdered in the UFC."

-On internet fighting sensation Kimbo Slice

ANTI-DUMB COMPETITION

"I think it's ridiculous. People think we're anti-competition? We're anti-dumb competition. Putting a 50-year-old guy in the Octagon for the first time and then putting out a press release like it's a big deal. Are you serious?"

-On Strikeforce announcing they had signed NFL great Herschel Walker

TRUE OR FALSE

"I just heard that there was another absolutely fucking retarded story written by Loretta Hunt. Loretta, you fucking moron, it has always been the policy at the UFC that the fighters get so many credentials and they can credential whoever the fuck they want... maybe you're the liar writing bullshit fucking stories. Everything that comes out of your mouth is fucking stupid...hey Loretta, if you're going to write a story, you fucking moron, at least make sure it's fucking true and you have some facts and if you're going to put some fucking quotes in there, get some quotes from people who at least have the fucking balls to put their fucking name on it...you fucking dumb bitch. Fuck you, Loretta Hunt."

-Responding to an article written by Loretta Hunt, News Editor for Sherdog.com

TRUE OR FALSE II

"The story that was written was so dumb, and so moronic and so amateur. The story is as false as false can be and everyone inside the industry knows it."

-Responding to an article written by Loretta Hunt, News Editor for Sherdog.com

TRUE OR FALSE II

"...Jake Rossen, what he likes to do is, he likes to write bullshit stories smashing MMA and MMA writers so that you, the fans, will go on there and talk about it for a long time. Typical fucking, douche bag reporter. Jake Rossen, go fuck yourself."

-Responding to an article by MMA writer, Jake Rossen

BILLBOARD ADVERTISING

"There's a billboard of his big ugly gorilla face at the busiest point in Las Vegas, where it can scare kids who are riding by in their cars."

-On Tito Ortiz adorning a UFC billboard

SMALL-TIME

"They want to fight me, we're gonna fight. You know how that goes and you know how that ends. They're a small-time show that's trying to act big. It's a joke. It's a tiny little regional show with nobody in it..."

-On rival MMA promotion, Strikeforce

T-SHIRT GUYS

"The guy sells t-shirts for a fucking living and now he wants to be a promoter? A t-shirt guy doesn't know what he doesn't know about this business yet…. He's going to find out, though."

-On Affliction Vice-President Tom Atencio promoting MMA

T-SHIRT GUYS II

"I don't like these guys and I want to see them spend more of their t-shirt money… what they need to start worrying about is nobody wants to wear their goofy fucking clothes anymore. The fad is over so they better start saving as much of that t-shirt money as they can."

-On Affliction's clothing line

FROM RUSSIA WITH LOVE

"It's basically them coming and saying, 'We've got this guy and some people say he might be the best heavyweight in the world. So for that, we want half your business.' Yeah, OK. That shit probably works in Russia, not here."

-On Fedor Emelianenko's management

FROM RUSSIA WITH LOVE II

"He's got nutty managers. These guys are from Russia, coming to America trying to strong-arm us into some deal we don't want to do. Go do that to the butcher down the street in Russia. It won't work over here in the United States."

-On Fedor Emelianenko's management

RINKY-DINK

"I'm not talking about one of these little, rinky-dink upstarts. These two companies you keep talking about are rinky-dink upstarts. They don't even really exist."

-On the now defunct MMA promotions the IFL and Elite XC

DONE

"He's one of the most dishonest human beings I've ever met. I put up with him when he was a good fighter. He's not anymore. He's done. I'm no longer in the Tito Ortiz business."

-On Tito Ortiz

GOT GAME

"EA doesn't give a fuck about Mixed Martial Arts."

-On Electronic Arts' new MMA video game

NEWSWORTHY

"It's actually fucking hilarious that that would be big news, that a guy who hasn't won a fight in over two years is signing a major deal. You mean to tell me that I can put some money down and I can see Babalu and Tito, both the guys that got knocked out twice by Chuck Liddell, fight each other. That's fucking entertaining."

-On Tito Ortiz reportedly signing with Affliction

BEAT HIM OFF

"This ain't fucking Survivor where we fucking vote him off, we'll beat him off."

-On TUF contestant Junie Browning

PREMONITION

"Urijah Faber is 145 pounds. He'll beat Kimbo Slice. Kimbo Slice sucks. He's terrible. If I had a heavyweight 'The Ultimate Fighter' show, I don't think he'd win the show. And he's headlining a show on CBS?"

-On Kimbo Slice

NASCAR

"All these other guys blew their brains out and spent millions and millions of dollars that if done the right way, they could have made money and built the business. But no, we're going to go out and compete with the UFC. You know how fucking dumb that is? It's like us sitting at my house on a Sunday going, 'Look at this NASCAR. Oh, my God. Look at all the people there. Look at how much money they're making. You know what? We should steal a couple of their drivers, and we'll start our own league.' Does that sound fucking dumb to you? That's how fucking dumb it is to think you're going to come out and compete with us now."

-On rival MMA promotions

REFEREES

"Mazzagatti will fuck up any fight. The worst referee in the history of fighting, period. The guy has no business watching Mixed Martial Arts, let alone refereeing it."

-On UFC referee Steve Mazzagatti

BALLROOM BLITZ

"These guys from K-1 are coming in and telling you, 'we're gonna sell out a 100,000 seat arena.' You idiots, you can't sell out a ballroom in Las Vegas."

-On now defunct MMA promotion, K-1 Hero's

PRAYER

"Talk to God and let him give you the day off to come watch."

-On religious MMA fans not wanting to watch the UFC on a Sunday

KIMBO SUCKS

"Ken is way past his prime, it gets to the point where it's dangerous for that guy to still be fighting, that being said, he still might beat Kimbo. Kimbo sucks."

-On the Kimbo Slice vs. Ken Shamrock match-up

CRAZY RUSSIANS

"Fedor's managers are crazy Russians who only care about themselves."

-On Fedor Emelianenko's managers

DOLLARS AND SENSE

"Tito Ortiz...He's a moron, a complete and total moron. His whole career, he's stepped over a dollar to pick up a dime. I'm sick of him. It's time he started beating up someone other than a nearly 50-year-old Ken Shamrock."

-On Tito Ortiz

BUILT THIS SPORT

"I built this sport off all the things I thought were wrong with boxing."

-On the difference between the business models of the UFC and boxing

DIVE

"...I'm flattered that we make it look that easy but this is a rough business. How many companies got to sink and lose twenty, thirty million dollars before these morons start to realise you just don't dive in..."

-On rival MMA promotions

MILLIONAIRES

"I've made more millionaires in the last eight years than anybody in the history of Mixed Martial Arts."

-On UFC fighters salaries

PIE

"They don't care about Mixed Martial Arts, these fucking jerk offs are in it for the money, these guys want to come in, take a piece of the pie and they don't give a fuck if they destroy the whole sport."

-On Elite XC Management

EXPERIENCED

"Let me tell you what; I've been in this business for a long time. Nobody, and I mean fucking nobody, knows more about this business than I do."

-On the MMA business

CHECK MATE

"We've created a business where 15 years from now Chuck Liddell can still be making money on royalty checks...I can tell you this right now; Leon Spinks isn't collecting any checks..."

-On the UFC's business model

KEEPING IT REAL

"There's a small amount of people that want to see a freak show and there's a ton of people that want to see a real sporting event."

-On the evolution of the UFC

KEEPING IT REAL II

"This isn't the WWE. I don't ask these guys to act crazy so we get more pay-per-views. That's not the business I'm in."

-On Brock Lesnar's post fight antics at UFC 100

UNBALANCED

"Tito couldn't balance his check book."

-On Tito Ortiz reportedly trying to start a fighters union

FAVORITE FIGHT

"Matt Hughes vs. Trigg 2 is my favorite fight ever…I mean MMA, boxing, pea-knuckle, I don't care what you're talking, I mean my favorite fight."

-On Matt Hughes and Frank Trigg's second fight

A FICTION

"The guy's a loser, anything this guy has ever said, has never come true...and we're going to listen to what he has to say?"

-On Affliction Vice-President, Tom Atencio

TWO CONTRACTS

"We've decided there is no loser in this fight and we're gonna offer Stephan Bonnar a six-figure contract with the UFC."

-After 'The Ultimate Fighter 1 Finale' bout between Stephan Bonnar and Forrest Griffin

GOING GLOBAL

"We got in this thing because we love this sport, we love the UFC, and we have this vision to take this thing globally and turn it into the biggest sport in the world."

-On the future of the UFC

READY TO GO

"We're very excited, we got a sell out crowd here of 5000 people, revved and ready to go."

-At UFC 30, his first ever show as UFC President

END GAME

"Here's what I believe; I'm the guy with the road map. I'm the guy who knows where I want to go with this thing. I know what my end game is. I know where it is...When this thing is a sport, all over the entire world, and you can take the UFC to any city in any country, just like soccer, then I did it. I did what I set out to do. That's why I was put on this planet. That's my job, my destiny, whatever the fuck you want to call it."

-On the future